Aim for a Star

Aim for a Star

HELEN LOWRIE MARSHALL

Doubleday & Company, Inc.   Garden City, New York

To My Friends

"He who aims highest
will reach the loftiest
ideal."

—Farrar

ISBN: 0-385-08258-4
Library of Congress Catalog Card Number 64–14800
Copyright © 1964 by Helen Lowrie Marshall
All Rights Reserved
Printed in the United States of America

9 8 7 6

Contents

5

Aim for a Star

Aim for a star! Never be satisfied
With a life that is less than the best,
Failure lies only in not having tried—
In keeping the soul suppressed.

Aim for a star! Look up and away,
And follow its beckoning beam.
Make each Tomorrow a better Today—
And don't be afraid to dream.

Aim for a star, and keep your sights high!
With a heartful of faith within,
Your feet on the ground, and your eyes
  on the sky,
Some day you are bound to win!

The Wonderful World Within

It's a wonderful world we call our Self,
  Wide as our love is wide,
High as our hopes that ride the sky,
  Deep as our faith's deep tide.

A constantly new, exciting world
  With vast lands yet unmapped,
Great veins of undiscovered ores,
  Resources still untapped.

A world that lures the venturesome
  To seek its wealth untold,
To penetrate its forest depths,
  To bring to light its gold.

A wonderful world we call our Self—
  Wide as our love is wide,
High as our hopes that ride the sky,
  Deep as our faith's deep tide.

Look Up and Live

This business of living was meant to be more
   Than plodding along each day
With head bowed down and eyes on the ground
   While Time ticks the hours away.

God made this world a delightful place
   With beauty everywhere—
The grass, the flowers, the trees, the sky,
   The tang of clean, fresh air—

A world to be lived in, laughed in, loved,
   To be met with joy and zest,
A world with a challenge for each of us
   To give it our very best.

This business of living was never meant
   As a treadmill sort of thing;
There are rivers to cross, and mountains to climb,
   And glorious songs to sing!

Around the Bend

We never know what waits around the bend;
The Master Planner must have planned it so,
That we may fully savor each day's blend
Of happiness and sadness as we go.

For even joy's full flavor would be lost
Were it not given us in morsel size;
And sorrow would exact too great a cost,
Were not tomorrow's pain screened from our eyes.

There is a comfort comes with each day's end,
A hope that clings to things beyond our sight.
We never know what waits around the bend—
It is enough that dawn shall follow night.

I Looked for God

I looked for God to be revealed. I thought
Now will some wondrous miracle be wrought;
Some mystic sign will surely now appear
To prove beyond a doubt that God is near.

But life went on in much the usual way;
Familiar homely tasks absorbed each day.
No mystical experience was mine;
No evidence of miracle divine.

But, gradually, with heart alert to see,
His signs in simple things were shown to me.
I saw Him in my house, fresh-cleaned and bright;
I saw Him in my sleeping child at night.

I felt Him kneel beside me in my garden;
At close of day I knew His peace and pardon.
I looked for God and found Him all about—
No miracle—just peace replacing doubt.

More Time to Live

We ought to take more time to live—
　　More time to really see
The glory and the wonders of this earth;
The quiet, gentle beauty,
　　The sheer nobility
Revealed alone to those who prize its worth.

We ought to take more time to care—
　　To really, truly care,
Enough to fling our heart's door open wide;
To lend a helping hand and share
　　The burdens others bear,
And take the poor and comfortless inside.

We ought to take more time to feel—
　　To surely, deeply feel
The quiet depth and power of God's love;
The close-enfolding presence of His peace,
　　Profound and real,
The faith that lifts the soul to heights above.

We ought to take more time to live—
　　To wholly, truly live,
More time to feel and care, more time to see;
To fully realize the endless joys
　　That life can give,
To laugh—and love—and live abundantly!

A Moment of Quiet

We say grace before meals at our house;
It's a custom we like because,
Out of the rush of the busy day
It gives a moment's pause.

A moment of quiet to realize
That God is with us yet,
A moment to count the blessings
We are so prone to forget.

We ask the blessing at our house,
And that quiet moment of peace
Brings to the tensions of the day
A gentle, sweet release.

And Faith Is Born

Faith is not blind, unreasoning
Compliance, meekly given,
That somehow, somewhere there's a God
And somewhere there's a Heaven.

The honest mind will turn the facts—
The truth will bear the turning—
And faith is born within the heart
From yearning—yes, and learning.

Truly Blest

Have you felt that special stillness,
That solemn, reverent hush
That settles on the earth
   At close of day;
As though the world had come to rest
In all its frenzied rush
And paused for one short moment
   Just to pray?

Have you sensed the awesome beauty,
The deep, pervading peace
That seems to fill the heart
   To overflow;
When all its pent-up love pours forth
In blessed, sweet release
Within that holy light
   Of evenglow?

If you've known this benediction,
Felt its calming in your soul,
Then you've come closer than
   You may have guessed
To the very gates of Heaven
Where you've been renewed, made whole,
And you have walked among those
   Truly blest.

Beyond Measure

How can one measure friendship—
The firm, warm clasp of a hand,
The comfort found in the welcome sound
Of the words, "I understand"?

How can one measure courage—
The strength we find to fight,
To suffer life's anxieties,
To stand up for the right?

How can one measure beauty, hope,
Or happiness, or love?
What man-made measure can encompass
Faith in God above?

So much of life—the best of life—
The things we truly treasure,
Are these, the gifts of boundless depth
Beyond all earthly measure.

Think and Be Glad

It's a busy world we live in,
  We get caught in the race,
And sometimes our sense of values
  Slips a little out of place.

It's a good thing to pull over
  To the roadside now and then
And get our thinking straightened out
  Before we start again.

And, like as not, we'll find a thought
  Or two to make us glad,
Some blessing that we've overlooked,—
  Forgotten that we had.

A few good honest thoughts and
  Chances are that we'll arrive
At the heartening conclusion
  That it's good to be alive.

There's a new exciting challenge
  In the race of life when viewed
With a heart refreshed with gladness,
  And with prayerful gratitude.

Not My Will

Against the door frame of my heart
I stood my soul. Its height I marked.
So small it was—so very small,
I thought if God could see at all
He'd understand it could not bear
Much suffering, or pain, or care.

But, though I knew that in God's eyes
I must appear of minute size;
Deaf to my pleas for leniency,
He heaped great burdens upon me;
And my poor soul was forced to bear
What seemed so much more than its share.

But, though it flinched, and flinched anew,
Somehow, (God must have known) it grew.
Each burden brought new strength, new height.
I often think how well it might
Be small and weak and helpless still,
If God had yielded to my will.

There Is a Strength

There is a strength
That comes through prayer,
A confidence, a power,
A quiet, deep, unflinching faith
To meet the trying hour.

There is a peace
That comes through prayer,
A calm serenity
To face whatever life may hold
With grace and dignity.

There is a joy
That comes through prayer,
A gladness of the soul,
A glorious sense of having been
Refreshed, renewed, made whole.

How—Not Why

Not why—dear God—
Please, let me not ask why
This bitter cup,
Nor spend myself
In futile questioning;
Let me look up—
Help me to face what is
And what must be,
Knowing Thou seest what
I may not see.

Not why—but how—
Lord, help me find the way
That this, my grief,
In some divine
And mystic manner may
Help my belief—
May mellow, strengthen,
Fortify my soul,
That I may better reach
Thine unseen goal.

Dear God—the clouds hang
Heavy in my sky—
Oh, give me grace to question
How—not why.

This I Know

Grief has its rhythm—first the wild,
Swift tide of dark despair;
The time of bleak aloneness,
When even God's not there.

And then the slow receding
Till quiet calms the sea,
And bare, washed sand is everywhere
Where castles used to be.

The gentle lapping of the waves
Upon the shore—and then
The pearl-lined shells of memories
To help us smile again.

There'll Be Another Spring

There'll be another spring, I know,
When flowers will replace the snow,
When birds will waken me at dawn
And pain and sorrow will be gone—
   There'll be another spring.

There'll be another day in June,
When, once more, life will be in tune,
When I will raise my eyes and see
A whole blue sky made just for me.
   There'll be another June.

And, till that June and springtime come,
I'll close my ears against the strum
Of wind and sleet upon the pane,
The cold, the loneliness—and then
   There'll be another spring.

I Know—I Know

Mary, whose Son was born so long ago,
How happy and how proud you must have been
To wrap your love around Him—watch Him grow—
I am a mother, too—that's how I know.

And when His baby hand let go your own,
How laughter must have mingled with your tears
To see Him stand and, wavering, walk alone—
I had a baby son—such joy I've known.

But oh, when you beheld Him dying there
Upon the cross, what terrible grief was yours,
Your Son, so young to die, so brave, so fair—
A warring killed my boy—I've known despair.

But then your Son arose—God's love to show—
What joy then must have filled your mother-heart
To know that He would live forever so—
My son is living, too—I know—I know.

Worthy of My Friends

If I could have but just one plea,
I think that that one prayer would be,
With all that such a prayer portends—
"Lord, make me worthy of my friends.

Help me to be the kind of man
That loyal friends believe I am.
Help me to be as true and fine
As they believe—these friends of mine.

Give me the courage under stress
That they expect me to possess;
And when they smile and look at me,
Oh, let me *be,* Lord, what they see!

Help me all pretense to forego,
And simply, without pomp or show,
Repay with true sincerity
The loyal faith they have in me.

And if, sometimes, I may have erred,
In any thought or deed or word,
Then help me, Lord, to make amends—
Lord, make me worthy of my friends."

These Are the Days

These are the days—these autumn days,
  When memories haunt us most;
When our Yesterday's Self goes wandering
  Like a restless little ghost
Down long-forgotten pathways
  Of things that used to be,
Vainly trying to fasten leaves
  Back on a bare-blown tree.

These are the days—these leaf-strewn days,
  When poignant hours we've known
Toll the heart's most solemn bell
  With deep and mournful tone;
When restless yearnings bare the soul
  As fall winds bare the trees,
Till, lonely and alone, it stands,
  A prey to winter's breeze.

These are the days—these frost-filled days,
  For which the spring was born,
For which the summer gave her bloom—
  The evening of the morn.
These are the days—these sere, brown days,
  When man is given to see
The cycle of the universe
  And his own destiny.

But oh, these, too, are golden days,
  With beauty unsurpassed—
Days when our life brings forth its yield
  Of riches from the past;
Days when the golden wealth of joys
  And tears that we have sown
Has reached its ripe fruition—
  To strength and beauty grown.

These are the days—the harvest days,
  When life is rich and whole—
The spirit's golden bounty days,
  Fulfillment of the soul.

I Know

You say there is no proof that God exists;
'Tis but a supposition—no-one knows.
Oh, but you're wrong, my friend, so very wrong.
There's proof enough. I know. I've seen a rose.

Take My Hand

Are you troubled, burdened, blue?
  Take my hand.
I've been troubled, burdened, too,
  I understand.
Where you've fallen, once I fell—
Oh, I know these pitfalls well.
Let me help the clouds dispel—
  Take my hand.

Others helped when I was weak,
  Took my hand,
Helped me face toward the peak,
  Helped me stand.
What they did, now let me do—
Pass that kindness on to you.
Some day you'll help others, too.
  Take my hand.

Old Cultures

This, then, is Yesterday, as I recall—
A slower pace, a calmer frame of mind,
A far more peaceful picture, all in all,
Than in Today's mad whirlwind man can find;
A picture full of quaint, God-fearing folk
With mirth-provoking, rough, unpolished ways,
The butt of many a smart and social joke
Of those who would deride the 'good old days'.
But Time and Wisdom good bedfellows are—
Old cultures, scorned as having spent their worth,
Though but a candle pointing toward a star,
May yet become the savior of the earth;
    And Yesterday holds much man might well borrow
    To build a saner, happier Tomorrow.

Resurrection

        Great thoughts are like great men,
        Born to live and die—
        But resurrection robs the grave
        Where truth and greatness lie.

The dream precedes the deed—
  A boy must dream;
A youth must first see greatness
  In his scheme.
And, even though the dreaming
  Goes too far—
No one is hurt by reaching
  Toward a star.

And if the deed fall short?
  A little fall
Is better than no dream,
  No deed, at all.
The dream precedes the deed,
  And youth will find
That dreams are really windows
  Of the mind.

Consolation

Consumed with loneliness, my youthful heart
Condemned the fate that said we two must part;
Cried out, in deep self-pitying despair,
That such a tragic parting was unfair.

But one, the crown of wisdom on her head,
Spoke gently to my youth. "Hush, child", she said,
"And heed the word of one well past four-score—
Be glad you've someone to be lonely for."

Better Shared

Some things are better shared
  A grief, a joy,
A meal, an open fire,
  A book, a toy—
Yes, some things must be shared
  To fully please—
And our own faith is not
  The least of these.

Losers

That one you call a stranger,—
He calls you a stranger, too,
And yet you have the makings
Of a fine friendship, you two.

You have so many mutual likes
And dislikes, seems a shame
To miss it all because you
Just don't know each other's name.

But you think he should break the ice;
That's your place, he contends—
And so you both are losers
When you might have been good friends.

Legacy of Laughter

Life handed him a few hard knocks;
 Sometimes his luck was bad.
He had the usual ups and downs
 As most of us have had.

Grief had its day along his way,
 Great fortune passed him by,
But he always came out winner
 With a twinkle in his eye.

This legacy of laughter,
 A gift from some forbear,
Was all the weapon that he had
 To fight life's pain and care.

But he kept his sense of humor,
 And he laughed away the tears,
And he went on spreading chuckles
 All around him down the years.

And I know I'll find him waiting,
 When I join him by and by,
Likely joshing with the angels,
 With that twinkle in his eye.

Frontier Bride

She was not brave, nor unafraid. She came
Because she loved a man—the man whose name
She bore—whose children she would bear.
She only knew it was her lot to share,
For better or for worse, whatever fate
Might lie in wait for him, her chosen mate;
This man, whose rugged face turned toward the
    West,
Whose restless feet forever westward pressed,
Whose vision of a glorious Tomorrow
Bedimmed the journey's hardships, parting's sorrow.

And so she rode, with straight, proud, aching back,
Through heat and dust and Indian attack,
And hid her fear beneath a dainty bonnet,
The foolish bits of lace and ribbons on it
Mute testimony to that gentle life
Before she cast her lot as frontier wife.
And when, at last, they found their journey's end,
Long, lonely miles from relative or friend,
She made a home there on the prairie wild
And, unattended, brought forth her first child.

Through sickness, heartbreak, drouth and famine grim,
It was her love, her faith that strengthened him.
And if, at times, with toil and hardship pressed,
Her courage ebbed a little, no one guessed;
And if, upon her pallet in the night,
She shed a tear, she hid that tear from sight.
She was not brave, but some strength from above
Seemed to be vested in her life of love.

She plowed the fields, she baked the daily bread,
She nursed the sick, and helped lay out the dead.
She taught her children how to work and play,
To love the beautiful, to laugh, to pray—
And left to them the dainty little bonnet
With foolish bits of lace and ribbons on it—
A legacy of love and gentle pride
From her, who journeyed West—a frontier bride.

Never Alone

No man is whole unto himself;
    So much of him depends
On those in whom he puts his faith—
    His family, his friends,
The things that he believes in,
    His work, his rest, his play,
The ordinary happenings
    That go to make his day.
No man can ever stand alone,
    Nor need he so to stand,
For love is always very near,
    And God is close at hand.

The Little Fellow Who Fights

It isn't always the talented one
Who climbs to the greatest heights,
But the one who keeps going in spite of the odds—
The little fellow who fights.
For talent and genius are only as good
As the spirit that lies within,
And the one who hangs on with a stubborn grip
Is the fellow I'd pick to win.

Humdrum

Life gets a little humdrum
At certain times, that's true,
But I've a secret formula
I think might help you, too.

Just take the hum from the humdrum
And use it for humming a song,
And the drum for marking a stirring beat
In your heart as you march along.

Yes, life can get pretty humdrum,
It often does, alas,
But with humming and drumming you'll be surprised
How pleasantly time will pass!

Everybody Dreams

Everybody dreams—
The very young, the very old;
Everybody has a secret
Dream he's never told.
Everybody, at some time,
Has wished upon a star,
Blown out the candles on a cake,
Had hopes that drifted far.
Everybody dreams—
And dreams so often don't come true,
But I think life is better
For the dreams we have,

                    Don't you?

Truth Reflected

You are a mirror wherein I see
Myself—as I am, and as I should be.
I talk and you listen—that's all you do,
And yet I see in the eyes of you
The pattern of life fall into place—
The truth reflected in your face.

Spring

Pussy willows at my window,
Yellow crocus at my door;
Honeysuckle's fairly bustin',
Give it just a few days more.

Tulips pokin' up green fingers
Jest to test the time o' year;
Aim to keep their heads well covered
Till they're sure Spring's really here.

Not so cautious, Mr. Robin;
First warm springlike breeze that blows,
There he is, his brown head bobbin'—
Where he comes from, no-one knows.

Calling Card

Spring came last night on tiptoe
When all the world was still.
Though Winter pelted her with snow,
She left one daffodil—
One golden daffodil she left
Before she ran away—
One daffodil to let us know
That she'd be back one day!

Tomorrow

Tomorrow does not stand apart,
  A shining, all new day;
Tomorrow is a thing slow-built
  Of hours passed away.

It's made of dreams your heart has stored,
  And dreams discarded, too;
It's made of all the joys and tears
  The years have brought to you.

It's made of lessons you have learned,
  The friends you've known,—the foes;
As each of our Todays is bent,
  So our Tomorrow grows.

It's made of sweat and toil and pain
  And song and love and laughter;
Each minute of Today helps build
  The day that follows after.

Tomorrow does not spring full-built
  With some new dawn's bright rays—
Tomorrow is a slow-built thing
  Made up of Yesterdays.

Point of View

A weighty problem might be
Likened to a mountain tall,
With you and I sincere
In our belief we see it all,
When actually, we only see
The side within our view.
Small wonder you're at odds with me,
And I at odds with you.

But if I make an effort
To cross over to your side,
And if you, too, sincerely try
To scale the Great Divide,
We're bound to find there at the peak
A common meeting place
Where we can see each other's side
As we meet, face to face.

And problems, just like mountains,
Can be conquered if we do
Our best to reach the point
Where we can see the other's view.

The King in Him

I spoke to the beggar, the tramp in him;
He listened to all I said,
Silent, surly submission
Portrayed in his low-bowed head.

Another spoke to the king in him,
And his bowed head sprang erect,
And I saw his eyes as his hidden pride
Responded to respect.

We both asked the selfsame favor,
But mine was the shame in the end.
My order was filled by a grudging slave;
While his was a gift from a friend.

I Saw an Artist

I saw an artist at work today,
He had no paint and he had no clay,
And his hands were rough and his shop was worn,
But he was an artist truly born,
For his work was exacting and fine and true
As he carefully mended a worn-out shoe.

Bargain a Bit

Bargain a bit with that dream of yours
   Before you abandon it;
There may be conditions that must be met,
   You've never quite dared to admit.
Bring it down out of the distant blue
   And tether it firm to earth;
Look at it squarely, man to dream—
   Measure its honest worth;
Then bargain a bit, give a little more time,
   If you must, a concession or two.
Any dream worth the dreaming deserves
   A generous chance to come true!

Two Words

Two words there are that have the power
To lighten man's most trying hour;
Two words, the heart's deep, silent song
When shadows lengthen weary-long;
Two words that carry hope's bright ray—
Two little words—"Some day! Some day!"

Legacy

I never give a penny,
No pet charities have I;
I choose to leave a legacy
Of some worth when I die.

I never give, but I invest
As wisely as I can,
And you're correct in thinking
I'm a very selfish man.

For my investments pay me well,
Their dividends are high.
For every dollar I invest,
A richer man am I.

For I invest in children's smiles,
And old folks' happiness,
And youngsters who are starting
Up their ladder to success.

And I share in the business
Of my Partner in the Sky.
We talk each matter over,
Each investment, He and I.

He helps me see the hidden worth
Of lives my path may cross,
And then we work together
To bring profit out of loss.

I never give, I just invest;
A selfish man am I.
I hope to leave a legacy
Of real worth when I die.

The Greatest of These

Reason faces up to life,
And sees things as they are;

Hope sees things as they ought to be,
And wishes on a star;

Faith dreams of miracles to come
That only God can do;

Love goes to work with patient hands
To make these dreams come true.

Keep a Dream in the Making

Keep some little dream in the making
If youth you would like to hold.
Old Father Time is defeated by dreams—
A dreamer never grows old.

For dreams have a way of quickening
The heart, and the years pass you by.
You can always tell the man with a dream
By the ageless gleam in his eye.

So keep a small dream in the making.
It needn't be big or bold—
Just some little dream to beckon you on
And you'll never, no never, grow old.

Milestone

Today I baked a chocolate cake.
　I've done it times untold—
But this one marked a grim milestone,
　And suddenly I'm old.

A birthday cake? Oh no, not that,
　But this cake is the one
That's always been the favorite
　Of my gangling teenage son.

He's always hung around to "help",
　Complete with running chatter,
Then scraped the bowl to get the last
　Rich smidgeon of the batter.

And now, today, this shock that brought
　To focus speeding years—
(I fussed with dishes at the sink
　To hide my foolish tears.)

The cause of all this inward pain,
　This anguish in my soul?
Today my son became a man—
　He didn't lick the bowl.

The Girls

She's lunching with 'the girls' today;
   She has a new spring hat.
She'll have a lovely time, I know,
   The 'girls' will see to that.

They'll all talk simultaneously
   Of politics and clothes,
And calories and cleansing creams
   And recipes and shows.

They'll brag on their grandchildren
   And state decided views
On what the President should do
   About the latest news.

They'll criticize new hairstyles,
   TV and movie stars,
And argue pro and con the chance
   We'll ever get to Mars.

Inconsequential chatter?
   Perhaps, but then again
Such woman-talk's elixir
   To one past three-score-ten.

And, birthdays notwithstanding,
  Their curtain's far from rung—
As long as they're 'the girls' their hearts
  Will stay forever young.

Her new spring hat is pert and gay
  Atop her soft grey curls.
She'll have a lovely time today—
  She's lunching with 'the girls'.

Now, Why Didn't I Think of That?

I have a second self in me
That people scarcely ever see—
A very charming, clever chap
Who has no tongue-tied handicap;
Who always has a quick come-back,
Smart repartee, a cute wisecrack.
The only trouble is that he
Speaks only when alone with me.
All night his wit flows through my head—
The brilliant things I wish I'd said.

Just Plain Fate

I always try to keep myself
Well groomed and clean and neat—
I always am—except when
Some old beau I chance to meet.

I pride myself on keeping
My house trim as a pin—
It always is—except the day
My mother-in-law drops in.

The cakes I bake are wonderful,
(Or I'd be ten pounds thinner!)
But they invariably collapse
When guests are due for dinner.

I could go on for hours.
Although I live by rule,
There's always that exception
That makes me out a fool.

They say the law of averages
Should keep the balance straight,
But in my case it doesn't work—
With me, it's just plain Fate.

I Go Buy-Buy

A bargain-hunting addict,
That's me—I can't deny it.
Show me a tag marked "Price Reduced"
And on the spot I buy it.

Though nine times out of ten
It's something I don't need at all—
A bird cage when I have no bird,
A damaged parasol,

A set of saucers without cups,
A shopworn last-year's bonnet—
It's not the article, itself,
It's that "Reduced Price" on it.

A bargain basement lures me
Like a magnet down its stairs,
And oh, the way I gloat and drool
At its enticing wares!

And oh, the glow I feel when I
Bring home my damaged treasure!
But, really now, what other sport
Can give such harmless pleasure?

I know it's just a habit,
But I've no wish to be weaned.
I'm a bargain-hunting addict,
A bargain-basement fiend.

The Packrat Moves Up

We have a new house. It's a model
Of cleancut, efficient compactness,
  Not an inch of waste space,
  Everything in its place,
Adhered to with rigid exactness.

Our architect frowned on a basement;
Quite patiently he pointed out
  There was no need at all
  For that monstrous catch-all—
What it held we could well do without.

With shame we considered that jumble
Of boxes, old trunks, dusty shelves;
  Every cranny and spot
  Filled with Heaven knew what—
We'd even forgotten, ourselves.

There were old magazines we were saving
To read on some vague rainy day,
  And old photographs
  Only good now for laughs—
They really should be thrown away.

The camping equipment had lain there
Since Junior's Boy Scout expeditions;
  We could surely dispose
  Of Dad's old army clothes,
And Sister's eighth grade compositions.

Quite obviously, we concluded,
It was sheer sentimentality
  That had been in command—
  Now we'd take a firm hand
Get rid of it all, and be free!

So we voted thumbs down on a basement.
(The architect's joy was ecstatic!)—
  The stuff we kept there
  We now lug up a stair
And store in an unfinished attic!

And Now for the Weather Report

The weather's no fun any more
   The way it used to be.
Since Science took the guess-work out,
   It's dull as a, b, c.

No more can sudden showers bring
   Adventure in their train.
You can't pretend to be surprised—
   They said to look for rain.

No more need Uncle Ezra use
   His game leg to foretell
A big change in the weather.
   His leg might as well stay well.

There's no more speculation based
   On chattering of squirrels,
Or cattle grazing to the east,
   Or chimney smoke that curls.

They've got the situation well
   In hand. They know the score.
The weather can't surprise us
   But it's no fun any more.

The Chances Grandma Took

When Grandma was a bride
She went along her carefree way,
Quite unaware of man's
Most common enemy today.

In blissful ignorance she baked
Her puddings and her pies.
She never heard of calories—
Those demons in disguise.

She blithely went ahead
And served her three square meals a day,
And ate them, too, without a thought
Of what the scales would say.

Hot biscuits every meal with jam,
Rich cakes, delicious pies,
Potatoes, luscious shortcake
With whipped cream to the skies!

It makes me shudder when I think
What chances Grandma took;
Without a thought for calories—
The things she used to cook!

It also makes me furious
Why I can't even squeeze
Into Grandmother's wedding dress—
And I count calories!

Christmas Star

He's the littlest Cherub on the right,
  The one with the wings askew;
His halo's slipped a little bit—
  (Most small boys' halos do!)

It's hard for him to stand so still—
  He stoops to scratch his knee.
He's not a bit afraid, though;
  I'm the nervous one—not he!

See how his eyes go roaming?
  Now they meet mine with a wink,
And sudden tears so fill my own
  That I can only blink.

I know I'm being foolish,
  But this play's his very first,
And I don't mind admitting
  I'm so proud that I could burst!

There are dozens in the pageant,
  More important parts, by far,
But not one can hold a candle
  To my own small Christmas Star!

As Long As There Is Christmas

As long as there is Christmas,
As long as children sing
The ageless carols heralding
The birthday of the King;
As long as Christmas bells ring sweet
And clear upon the air,
And hearts are filled with loving
And an eagerness to share;
As long as there are Christmas trees
And candles on the sill,
And one day in the year touched with
The magic of good will;
As long as there is Christmas—
Oh, surely it must be
That peace is not beyond the realm
Of possibility.

I Wonder

She looked toward the Eastward,
She, who had given birth
To Him, who brought love to mankind
And peace—goodwill on earth.

I wonder, did her mother-eyes
See, through her tears of joy,
A cross, where others saw the star
That heralded her Boy?

Merry Christmas, Everybody!

There's no-one who enjoys the Christmas
    Season more than Father.
He calmly holds himself aloof
    From all the fuss and bother.
Good will's the order of the day—
    He'll tolerate no other!
The trying details, cheerfully,
    He relegates to Mother.

He's never quite outgrown his days
    Of Santa Claus believing;
The effort Mom expends is simply
    Past his mind's conceiving.
For him the tree springs into bloom,
    All fully trimmed and glowing;
Just how it got its glitter,
    He's not interested in knowing.

The gay, beribboned packages,
    Appear as if by magic—
To disillusion him right now
    Would be just short of tragic!
The Christmas cards go out on time.
    His friends all understand
He's thinking of them, even though
    They are in Mother's hand.

The fruitcake and the Christmas sweets
      Are there, his to enjoy—
They've always been there, ever since
      He was a little boy.
It never enters his sweet head
      That somebody or other
Must manage all of this—oh, no,
      He leaves that up to Mother.

No sir, there's no-one who enjoys
      The Christmas Season more—
And, since he gets the bills, perhaps
      That evens up the score.

Christmas

   Merry songs and holly wreathes
   And softly drifting snow—
   Candle light and Christmas trees
   And children's eyes aglow;
   A glory and a sadness all mixed up
   Inside the heart,
   And a loving there so fierce
   That it tears the soul apart—
   That's Christmas.

Once on a Star-Filled Night

Once on a star-filled night long years ago,
Beneath a sky so bright it seemed to glow,
Within a stable crude where cattle slept,
A little Boy was born—a promise kept.

A little Boy was born to walk the earth
And teach the world the power and the worth
Of love—to show how wars might ever cease
And man might live with man—a world of peace.

A little Boy, whose tiny fingers curled
Around His mother's, would remold the world.
A little Boy whose life would grow to be
The model life for such as you and me.

A little Boy who, long before His prime,
Would make the final sacrifice sublime,
And leave the world far richer for its loss—
For this He was to die upon the cross.

Once, on a star-filled night long years ago,
A mother lulled her Baby soft and low—
I wonder, did she sense the awful shame—
A world so soon forgetting why He came?

Very Special Night

Once there was a little angel
Kneeling by a manger bed,
With her chubby fingers folded
And a halo 'round her head.
And her wings were edged in tinsel,
And her gown was long and white,
And her hair was curled in ringlets
For this very special night.

And she saw the barefoot shepherds
Keeping watch with cardboard sheep,
And she heard the angel chorus
Wake the shepherds from their sleep.
And she watched the bathrobed Wisemen,
The "three Kings from Orient-tar,"
Place their gifts before the manger—
A gold box, some beads, a jar.

And she saw the bright star shining
From the choir loft up high,
And she heard the choir singing
Just like angels in the sky.
And her eyes were round and solemn,
And her fingers folded tight—
And there'll never be another
Half so beautiful a night.

Christmas Eve in the Morning

It's Christmas Eve in the morning
Exactly a quarter to seven,
When out of their beds and onto ours
Come bouncing our bundles from Heaven.
  Bubbling with pre-Christmas spirit,
  They pelt us with question balls.
  "Will Santa be flying a Jet this year?"
  And "What if his engine stalls?"
"Wouldn't a helicopter
Be better for landing on roofs?"
"Silly, he uses a parachute,"
Our eldest solemnly spoofs.
  Later in robes and pajamas
  We dole out the morning mush,
  And thank the Lord for the quiet
  That comes in that moment's hush
When the grace is said, and each small head
Is bent in reverent respect;
For, sure as you're born, as on every morn
I know what next to expect!
  It's "Amen"—Go!—and from then I know
  It's every man for himself.
  This time, it's true, something's added
    that's new—
  Talk of the whiskered old Elf.

The baby tips over her mug of milk,
And Junior plays drum with his spoon,
While all join in with a whoop and a din
In a rollicking Christmas tune.
  Above and beyond the confusion
  I patiently try to reason—
  It's not the Old Nick they're full of today,
  It's only Saint Nick and the Season.
As soon as I can, I bundle them up
In leggings and mittens and boots
And shoo them all out to play in the snow
'Ere my nerves shatter clean to their roots!

  But in the calm and the quiet,
  As I finish trimming the tree,
  And wrap up the last Christmas present,
  I'm awfully glad that I'm me.
I'm glad that they call me "Mother"—
That small bunch of hellions outside,
And I watch them snowballing each other
With a warm glow of love and of pride.
  It's Christmas Eve in the morning,
  And life runs its hectic pace—
  But just for the moment all I can recall
  Are those small heads bowed for grace.
And I pause for a silent minute,
And my heart says a "Thank You" prayer
For this wild and wonderful family of mine
And for families everywhere.

61

I Would Keep Christmas

This year I would keep Christmas,
Would hold it fast and keep
This miracle of love within my heart;
Would let its warm, life-giving glow
Through all my being seep
Till it becomes of me a living part.

I would hold its beauty
And its wonder in my eyes,
Have them reflect its sparkle and its cheer;
Would keep my ears attuned
To angel voices in the skies,
Would have my heart sing carols all the year.

This year I would keep Christmas,
Would have its guiding star
Lead me toward the Christ Child and His way,
Would show that light to others
Who are traveling from afar
And make each day a blessed Christmas Day.

Christmas Prayer

Give us this day—this Christmas Day,
This day of Thy sweet birth,
A tongue to tell its beauty,
A heart to count its worth,
A hand to show its meaning,
A will its peace to share,
A love that reaches out to all
Thy children everywhere.

This Is the Day We Put Christmas Away

This is the day we take down the tree
    And put all the tinsel away,
The glittering balls, the twinkling lights,
    Awaiting next year's holiday.

This is the day we take down the wreath,
    The mistletoe hung overhead,
The garlands and festoons, the candles, the cards,
    The Babe in His manger bed.

Yes, this is the day we put Christmas away—
    But oh, not its warmth and its cheer.
Let these be the candles we keep in our hearts
    To light our way all through the year.

Only Inches Away

Life is measured by inches,
By steps taken one at a time,
Not by the height of the peak we seek,
But each little rise we climb.

The span of our life is measured
Minute by minute—not years;
We live in a very small world of our own
In a vast universe of spheres.

Yes, life is measured by inches,
But inches can add up to far;
A light-year is only inches away—
We can inch our way up to a star!